LOOK!

MAKE OBSERVATIONS AND ASK QUESTIONS

Emma Carlson Berne

PowerKiDS press™

New York

Published in 2014 by The Rosen Publishing Group, Inc.
29 East 21st Street, New York, NY 10010

First Edition

Editor: Jennifer Way
Book Design: Kate Vlachos
Photo Research: Katie Stryker

Photo Credits: Cover © iStockphoto.com/PenelopeB; p. 4 wavebreakmedia/Shutterstock.com; p. 5 (left) York Black/arabianEye/Getty Images; p. 5 (right) mironov/Shutterstock.com; p. 6 (left) Goodluz/Shutterstock.com; pp. 6 (right), 7 iStockphoto/Thinkstock; pp. 8, 10 Ingram Publishing/Thinkstock; p. 9 uniquely india/Getty Images; p. 11 aodaodaodaod/Shutterstock.com; p. 12 Jupiterimages/Creatas/Thinkstock; p. 13 Katja Kircher/Maskot/Getty Images; p. 15 Monkey Business/Thinkstock; p. 16 Terrie L. Zeller/Shutterstock.com; p. 19 JGI/Jamie Grill/Blend Images/Getty Images; p. 20 Siobhan Connally/Flickr/Getty Images; p. 21 VStock/Thinkstock; p. 22 Popperfoto/Contributor/Getty Images.

Library of Congress Cataloging-in-Publication Data

Berne, Emma Carlson.
  Look! : make observations and ask questions / by Emma Carlson Berne. — First edition.
    pages cm. — (The scientific method in action)
  Includes index.
  ISBN 978-1-4777-2924-3 (library) — ISBN 978-1-4777-3013-3 (pbk.) —
  ISBN 978-1-4777-3084-3 (6-pack)
  1. Science—Methodology—Juvenile literature. I. Title.
  Q175.2.B473 2014
  507.2′4—dc23
                                      2013025979

Manufactured in the United States of America

CPSIA Compliance Information: Batch #WS14PK5: For Further Information contact Rosen Publishing, New York, New York at 1-800-237-9932

CONTENTS

WHAT IS THE SCIENTIFIC METHOD?

This scientist is looking at something using a microscope. Microscopes are tools used to see very tiny things.

A scientist is a person who studies why and how the world works. Scientists study plants, animals, air, the stars, and much more! A scientist is always asking questions and trying to find answers.

To find these answers, scientists do **experiments** using a plan called the **scientific**

method. The scientific method has six parts. The parts are making **observations** and asking questions, forming a **hypothesis**, planning an experiment, collecting information, **analyzing** the results, and sharing the results.

In this book, we will learn how to make observations like a scientist. To do this, we will have to look carefully at the world around us.

If you want to be a scientist, you have to look closely at the world around you. One way you could do this is to look at the stars through a telescope.

TOPICS OF INTEREST

Left: Do you like to go hiking with your family? If so, you could choose one plant you find on a hike to do an experiment on. *Right:* If you like baking cookies, you could test how using baking soda or baking powder changes how the cookies turn out. Always ask a parent or other adult to help you cook.

The scientific method starts with choosing a topic you want to **investigate** further. It can be hard to know just what you want to ask questions about. One way to choose a topic is to think about what you are interested in.

Health, animals, and nature are just a few of the many topics you could investigate.

After you think of an area you are interested in, you will want to **narrow** your topic down. For instance, if your topic is animals, pick one animal in which you are interested. Then you are ready to move on to the next step.

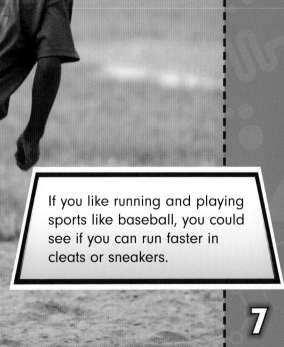

If you like running and playing sports like baseball, you could see if you can run faster in cleats or sneakers.

OBSERVING LIKE A SCIENTIST

"Observation" means "watching something very carefully." We look at things every day, but observing is different from just looking.

To observe something scientifically, you must watch very closely, look for the ways things **interact**, and find patterns. What happens in your neighborhood when it rains?

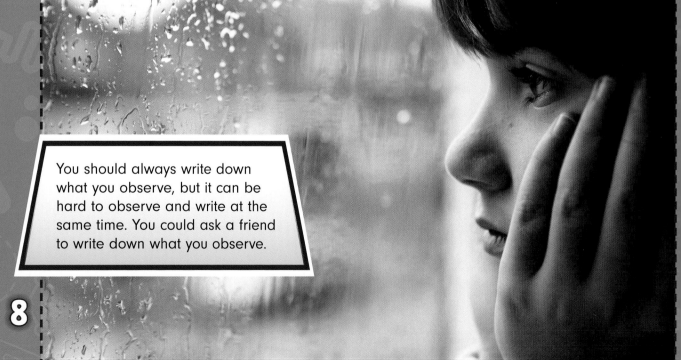

You should always write down what you observe, but it can be hard to observe and write at the same time. You could ask a friend to write down what you observe.

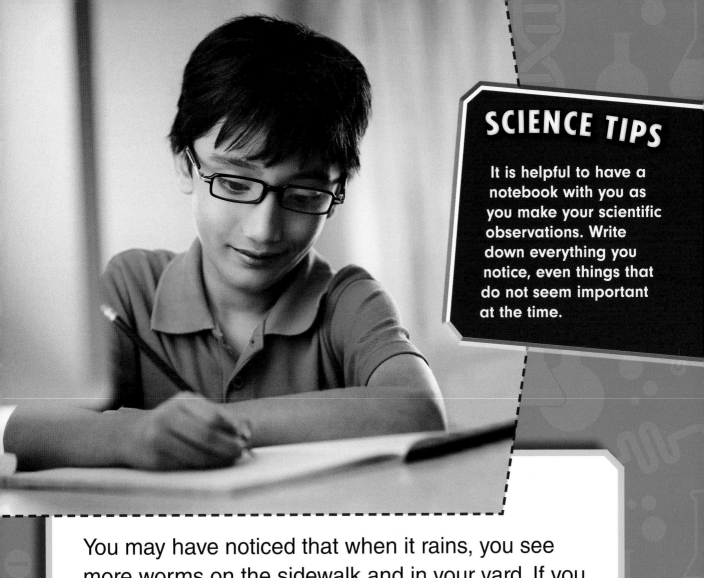

You may have noticed that when it rains, you see more worms on the sidewalk and in your yard. If you wanted to observe this, you would have to watch to see how many worms were above ground before it rains. How long do the worms stay above ground? Are they still there the next day?

EXPERIENCES ARE IMPORTANT

If your parents leave fruits and vegetables in a bowl on your table, you could observe them. Do some fruits and vegetables stay fresh longer than others?

Observations can come from your own **experiences**. Things that you see and do every day can be observed. You might have noticed that the day your parents bring home a bunch of bananas, the bananas are yellow and firm. In a couple of days, the bananas have brown spots and have softened. By the end of the week, any remaining bananas are brown and mushy. Why did the bananas become mushy, but the apple sitting next to them is still firm and red?

Many things in your daily life can be turned into observations. You just have to pay extra attention.

These bananas are for sale at a market. Knowing how long it takes bananas to turn brown and mushy can help you decide which bananas to choose and how many to buy.

USING YOUR SENSES

Observing is a type of looking, so you might think you just need your eyes. To observe, though, you should use all of your **senses**. Smell, touch, taste, and sound are all important observation tools. You can even observe things without seeing them. If you close your eyes and

This girl is smelling a flower. Try closing your eyes when you smell something. Does doing that help your sense of smell?

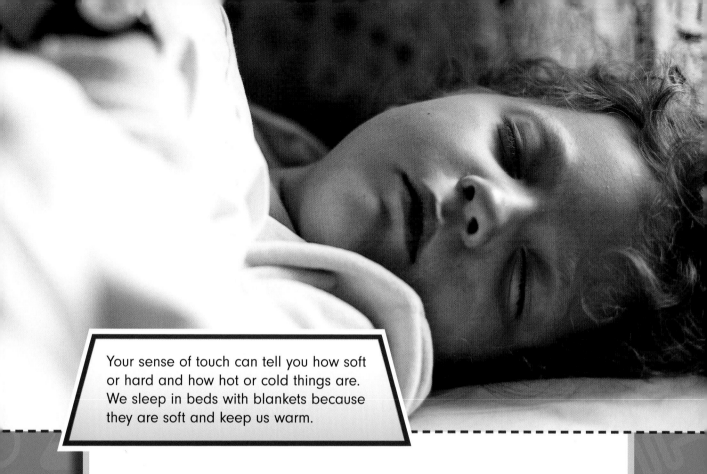

Your sense of touch can tell you how soft or hard and how hot or cold things are. We sleep in beds with blankets because they are soft and keep us warm.

take a bite of an orange piece, you can observe the way it tastes, the way it smells, and the way it feels in your hand. Do you feel the same sensations as strongly when you have your eyes open and eat the orange?

It is important to use as many senses as you safely can when observing. Using all your senses helps you make more detailed observations.

GET CURIOUS

Good scientists are curious about the world around them. Let yourself be curious about your observations. Curiosity is an important tool. The more curious you are about a topic, the more you will want to observe. The more you observe something, the more you will find yourself asking questions.

You have seen the changes in the bananas over the week and you may begin to wonder why they happen. Why do the bananas turn from yellow to brown? Why do they become mushy? Why don't apples become mushy as quickly? You can create a list of questions you have about your observations and then start researching to find answers.

SCIENCE TIPS

Be prepared to ask many more questions than you will wind up investigating. Eventually, you will weed out all the questions except one. That question will be the basis for your hypothesis.

This boy is creating a list of questions about the observations he has made. If he observed a fruit bowl, he might ask, Do grapes stay fresh longer than tomatoes?

15

Now that you've made an observation, you can turn it into a **scientific question**. This is a question that can be answered by measuring, observing, or experimenting. In other words, this is the question you're going to try to answer using the scientific method. Scientists also call this step stating the problem.

A good scientific question asks how one thing affects another thing. For instance, you might want to ask, Will bananas stay yellow and firm longer if they are in the refrigerator?

After observing flowers, you might ask a scientific question such as, Do flowers live longer when they are watered once or twice a day?

17

SORTING YOUR EVIDENCE

After you have an idea of what question you want to answer, you will need to sort through your **evidence**. What do you already know about your question? What do you need to find out? Other people may have already asked questions about this topic. Can you find their answers? Scientists often use the evidence of other scientists to help in their own experiments.

For instance, you already know that bananas will turn brown in about a week if left on the counter. You have evidence of that from your own observation. You want to know how fast they turn brown in the refrigerator.

You can find evidence from other scientists by reading books you find in the library. You can also search for evidence online using a computer.

If you are making daily observations during your experiment, you could record them in a calendar. A calendar is a good tool to use for the banana experiment.

Congratulations! You have done a lot of work so far. You have chosen a topic to investigate, made scientific observations, and asked questions. By this time, you may have an idea of what the answer to your question might be. If you have not, you might now have an idea of how to find the answer.

These thoughts will eventually help you form a hypothesis. The hypothesis is a statement about what you believe you will discover in your experiment. Then, you will try to prove your hypothesis is true by taking measurements and making observations during your experiment.

A ruler is a tool used to take measurements. If you wanted to test how fast flowers grow, you could use a ruler to measure the height of the flowers over time.

Scientists are always seeking to understand our fascinating, wonderful world even better. To do this, they are constantly making observations and asking questions. These observations and questions are the first steps to making important discoveries about the way nature and the universe work.

Many of the things we know about the world now started as observations. Long ago, people believed the Sun revolved around Earth. A scientist named Nicolaus Copernicus observed that Earth seemed to revolve around the Sun. Eventually, he proved that his observation was true.

Nicolaus Copernicus discovered that Earth and the other planets revolve around the Sun in 1543. This model of the universe is called a Copernican or heliocentric model.

GLOSSARY

analyzing (A-nuh-lyz-ing) Examining something carefully and thinking about what it means.

evidence (EH-vuh-dunts) Facts that prove something.

experiences (ik-SPEER-ee-ents-ez) Knowledge or skills gained by doing or seeing things.

experiments (ik-SPER-uh-ments) Tests done on things to learn more about them.

hypothesis (hy-PAH-theh-ses) Something that is suggested to be true for the purpose of an experiment or argument.

interact (in-ter-AKT) To act upon something else.

investigate (in-VES-tuh-gayt) To try to learn the facts about something.

narrow (NER-oh) To limit.

observations (ahb-ser-VAY-shunz) Things that are seen or noticed.

scientific method (sy-en-TIH-fik MEH-thud) The system of running experiments in science.

scientific question (sy-en-TIH-fik KWES-chun) The specific question you hope to find the answer to using the scientific method.

senses (SEN-sez) Taste, smell, touch, hearing, and sight.

INDEX

A
animal(s), 4, 7
answer(s), 4, 14, 18, 20
apple(s), 11, 14

B
bananas, 10–11, 14, 17–18

E
experiment(s), 4–5, 18, 21

H
hypothesis, 5, 14, 21

N
nature, 7, 22
neighborhood, 8

P
parents, 10
parts, 5
patterns, 8
plan, 4
plants, 4

R
results, 5

S
scientist(s), 4–5, 14, 17–18, 22
smell, 12
stars, 4
step(s), 7, 17, 22

T
touch, 12
type, 12

WEBSITES

Due to the changing nature of Internet links, PowerKids Press has developed an online list of websites related to the subject of this book. This site is updated regularly. Please use this link to access the list:
www.powerkidslinks.com/smia/look/